COVER1
AND D,

J

How to use Manipulation and Persuasion to
influence others and take control in personal
relationships (First Edition)

MARK SECRET

The information in the following pages is broadly considered a truthful and accurate account of facts and as such, any inattention, use, or misuse of the information in question by the reader will render any resulting actions solely under their purview. There are no scenarios in which the publisher or the original author of this work can be in any fashion deemed liable for any hardship or damages that may befall them after undertaking information described herein. Additionally, the information in the following pages is intended only for informational purposes and should thus be thought of as universal. As befitting its nature, it is presented without assurance regarding its prolonged validity or interim quality. Trademarks that are mentioned are done without written consent and can in no way be considered an endorsement from the trademark holder.

Table of contents

Chapter 1: What is the Difference between Manipulation and Persuasion?

Truly, these two concepts are very closely related and most of the people get confused between their differences and meanings and the line between them seems blurred. It is crucial for you to figure out when you are crossing the line of persuasion and entering into manipulation zone. Hence, before understanding what is the difference in them, let us first understand the meaning of them which would clear out the difference automatically.

Persuasion means when you say or act in such a way that people do or believe what you are saying. Persuasion is something that we do every day on a daily basis. Persuasion is never taken in evil or negative way. We can say that it is the way we interact with the people who are around us. At times while discussing any topic when we try to keep our point and prove ourselves right, that as well is persuasion. It also comes in picture when you want someone to do something right and want to see this world as a better place. Also, at times you try to persuade people when you want to earn a profit or sell a product and doing this is not being wicked or doing something immoral.

Let us understand this by taking an example when you make a product according to the customer's needs and requirements and want to make the journey of the buyer easy and then you are trying to convince them to buy it as you know it will benefit them and you both.

Now, let us understand what manipulation means. It means the act to change by unfair or artful means to serve your purpose. In manipulation, you are not bothered about the other person's benefit or less what you want to see is your revenue and benefit. In this case, you want your profit no matter what, by any means. If in case the buyer as well is benefiting then that is good but they are not concerned about that. Manipulation always comprises of deception and misrepresentation of the product or truth, but it does not go a long way.

Let us understand this as well by taking an example in relevance to the above-mentioned one. Here the company thinks of only their profit while making the profit irrespective of thinking about the customer needs and requirements. In such cases, the customer would only try the product once and when they will realize that it is not helping them or they have been deceived they would stop buying the product.

Most of the researchers say that the difference between the two comes down to basically three things which are-

a) The intention behind your persuasion

b) Transparency and truthfulness behind your desire

c) A benefit to the other person

•These were the major differences between persuasion and manipulation. Yes, there is a very thin line of intention between them, but it is important for you to realize it. Persuasion is always positive and manipulations are said to be negative and evil. With the help of persuasion in an argument, you try to make the interlocutor adopt your point of view, on the other hand, in manipulation; you bent the truth to get approval from the interlocutor. In persuasion, the opponent willing accepts your point but in manipulation, the person is coerced to agree.

•Persuasion is usually done with the intention to do good things. Here would try to recommend the buyer with the best services and try to make the perfect match and also would strive that the person stops using anything which is harmful. On the contrary in manipulation, only one of the parties is benefited

•In persuasion, you present all the right arguments in the best manner which are logical and convincing both but in manipulation people try to mould the truth so that they can achieve their selfish goals

•Although, in persuasion as well you try to convince others when they do not agree to your point. But the thing is that you are being transparent and the intentions are good and real. On the other hand, manipulation is opposite

•In persuasion, if the other person agrees to what you were trying to tell they would benefit by it as it was in their favor. But in manipulation, the other person would regret after agreeing to your point. The reason behind it is that the truth was not told, the customer had no benefit as the intent was never good.

I am sure by now it must be very clear to you that what does both these things mean and what are the major differences in them. Therefore, you should always think while convincing someone that does it benefit just you or the other person as well. It will become easy for you to understand whether you are doing something wrong or are you right.

Don't you think persuasion is a really good technique and every one of us should imply it in our lives and think about ours and others benefits too? So, let us learn a few persuasion tactics which would help you in changing other's mind-

•Scarcity Technique- This is the most used persuasion technique and mostly the salesman and marketers use it. I am sure that you must have seen that the product which is less in supply, people tend to ask more of it. Thus, if you want to increase the demand of your product or service always show that it is available for a limited time or the offer is just for the time being, it would increase the chances of increase in sales of your product. You must have read these lines many times such as never to be seen again, once a year, attaching a timer, limited offer, etc. Also, there was an experiment done where one group was given a product which was in great amount and the other group was given a product which was scarce. The end of this experiment was the second group could sell more products as people were keen to buy it because it was limited. You as well can use this tactic to increase the demand for your commodities.

•Social Authentication- People usually consider this technique as it does not take time to notice that in social groups people usually there are group thinkers of higher level. Whenever anyone thinks of a unique idea whatever everyone agrees or not but yes they think and give their point of view. So, whenever you will take any decision, in that regard you will always consider the points that your mates or friends mentioned. For example, there are many people who just start smoking either because for them it is social proof or their friends too so they also start doing it.

•Reciprocation- Most of the people like returning favors if someone does something good for them. Also, majorly people do not even know that they would like the gift or not they are just inclined to return the favor back. If you make someone feel indebted that is a good way increases the probability of getting what you desire. For example, you want to collect money for some old age people so that they can get a house. Instead of directly asking for money, according to their talent, you can ask them to make beautiful frames, pots, etc. Give them to people, make them feel indebted and then ask for a donation. Also, a study was done and seen the more kind the waiter was with the customers the more tip he got. So, be generous to all and they would in turn return generosity towards you.

•Authority- If you want to convince people always to show yourself as a source of authority. As most people look up to authority or a leader be it any field and get easily convinced when an authoritative person says something. For example, if you read that 9 out of 10 doctors recommend using a specific brand of soap, then most of the people would run after that brand as it has gained an advantage over others. This states that the majority of the people follow someone who has authority, at times even when they are wrong. This technique explains to you that always be confident and have your own attitude if you want people to follow you or get influenced by what you say or do.

•Regularity and commitment- It has been seen that people who show regularity and fulfill the promises then it helps them in influencing others to do more for them. Such as if you fulfill the commitment and do what you said in time, it influences others and make them believe that they can count on you and can help you in persuasion when you want them to do something for you. For example, many websites instead of writing signup, use the statement like- join me and the second option is No, I am boring. Statements like this convince customers and it increases their conversion rates.

•Foot in the door- This persuasion technique is very interesting and many people use it. This technique states that whenever you want a favor from someone, first ask for a smaller one and then ask for the bigger favor. It means that when you first ask for help and if the person says yes, they get committed to doing that and when you ask for the bigger help it can act as a continuation for the smaller one. For example, if you fail in a test and your teacher says no for taking the test again. You should first always ask for the feedback so that you can work on it. And then request the teacher whether they can take the test again. This way the teacher would see that you are really keen to learn and improve and would not say no.

•Door in the Face- Well, this technique has been seen in many stores and supermarkets. It is the opposite of the technique mentioned above. In this method, you first ask for big favors and if the person says no then request and ask if they can do something easy and small for you. This way the other person gets convinced and thinks that if not a big help but yes then can do a favor by doing something small. For example, you ask your cousin or any mate for Rs.10,000 if they say no then you can always say that if not 10,000 can you please help me with Rs. 3000? There are major possibilities that they would say yes.

•Anchoring- This is said to one of the most powerful persuasion methods. It has numerous uses but is mostly used in pricing. This technique can be best explained with the help of an example. You go to the market to buy a refrigerator for yourself, the salesman says Rs. 30,999 but you bargain and get the cost lowered to Rs.27,500. You would be happy that you got a great deal and feel satisfied, instead of knowing that the actual price of it was maybe less than that. But you are happy as according to you it was the best deal.

These were the best persuasion techniques which you can apply to your daily life if required as they are not manipulative but are very convincing and can also get your work done easily and quickly.

It is also prime for us to know some of the manipulator's emotional techniques and how to deal with them as they might be very difficult for you to point out if you are not aware of-

•No point coming in their words- Manipulators are wise enough to turn the statements that you say. Whatever you would say, they have explanations for everything and would turn the things around. For example, if they forget any special occasion and you complain them for it, they would always have explanation such as I am so sorry, I did not want to spoil your mood but I am having a bad

time at my work and was very much busy in it. If you think and it seems as the apology is fake, make sure that you do not come in their words. In such cases, always trust your intuition and if you feel it is fake, then do not accept the apology. Once you agree to it, then you will always be treated the same way.

•They pretend well that they want to help you- They are very good at faking out that they want to help you. They would at first say yes but make expressions that will show you that they are not willing to help you. And when you ask them if they do not want to help, then they would always pretend and say of course I want to help you and say how unreasonable you are. Ensure that if a manipulator says yes, held them accountable for it, do not buy their reasons. Make sure that if they do not want to do it they say it upfront, instead of saying yes to be in the good books.

•Dirty Fights- The worst part about them is that they would not fight directly with you, instead they would bitch around your back and ask others to convey the message as they would not want to deal with it directly. They would find different ways to let you know that they are not happy with you or not talking to you. First, they would show that they support you, but at the time of help, they would act weirdly. Such as they would ask you to study further and say that they support you but when you have exams they will call their friends for a house party. And when you fight with them on this they would have answers like life cannot stop, I have a life too. So make sure you make decisions on your own without being dependent as it can come back to you in a wicked manner.

•The impact the environment around them- They are so selfish that they just care about themselves and nothing else matters to them. When they are angry or do not get something that they wish for, they would change the climate around. The only way to fix it is to give them what they want to make them happy. But be careful, these people would let you forget your own needs and keep you busy with their requirements always. If you are with someone like this take a step back or think about the relationship again.

These kinds of behaviors are difficult to handle and escape, so be brave and bold if you are around people who are manipulators and take a step. Either face them or just ignore them, do not stay with them. Let us know more about the positives and negatives of these aspects in the next chapter.

Chapter 2: Covert Manipulation

Covert manipulation is as insidious as it sounds—it involves stripping power from another person so underhandedly and secretly that the individual who has lost power never realizes what has happened. A victim of covert manipulation may stop one day and realize she has no clue how her life has become what it is, feeling as though she is a stranger in a foreign land, with no idea how to act, communicate, or find her way home. She may find that her thoughts are no longer familiar to her, seeing them as entirely foreign to whatever she would typically believe. Even her behaviors no longer seem like the person she thought she was. Her sense of self, she has realized, no longer matches the person she has become.

Defining Covert Manipulation

Covert manipulation involves taking someone's innermost emotional vulnerabilities and using those identified vulnerabilities to manipulate a situation. The manipulator may incite fear, play with insecurities, or even convince an individual that he or she is losing touch with reality to sway the individual into following whatever it is that the manipulator desires.

Covert implies that this manipulation is hidden, or covert. This means that the manipulator is seeking to keep the manipulation within the boundaries of plausible deniability, which makes the manipulation that, much more insidious. If the manipulation is deniable, over time, the one being manipulated begins to doubt reality.

Manipulation implies that the individual being targeted is being swayed to do things that he or she would not ordinarily do, and when paired with being covert, the manipulation is done in ways that sway and control behaviors without the predator having to say exactly what is desired or expected.

People who have been covertly manipulated often describe it to being brainwashed, and to an extent, they were. They were changed over time without ever being aware of it happening. Those changes left the targets uncomfortable in their own skins and unsure how they ended up where they did or how they had possibly allowed themselves to be changed so much by someone else into someone unrecognizable and wondering how they never saw the warning signs that had to have been there somewhere.

How Covert Manipulation Works

Covert manipulation can be broken down into three steps that explain how it works and why. Each of these steps is critical and helps explain how covert manipulation works to deceive and influence individuals. First, the predator learns who the target is and works his or her way into the target's inner circle. The predator then begins to degrade away the target's sense of self, leaving behind a husk of a person that has been molded into something easily manipulated. Lastly, the predator is left with essentially a doll that can be toyed with and manipulated. The strings have been attached, and the manipulator is free to tug at them as he or she pleases, typically getting the desired result, and punishing when the desired result is not received.

Learning about Target

The first step of covert manipulation is to learn about the target. This stage may look as though the predator is interested in the target, and he is—but not genuinely. The predator is interesting in learning exactly how to get what he wants, not in getting to know what the other person is like.

This step typically involves getting to know what the target's family life was like, learning about friendships, sensitivities, belief systems, and your own personality type, in hopes of discovering any chips in your armor that is your self-esteem. The point of this step is to learn all about any weaknesses that may be able to be exploited at a later point in time.

This stage involves plenty of interaction with the target, which enables the manipulator to learn how to better read the individual's body language. Fears, strengths and weaknesses, worries, and even the target's hopes and dreams will be learned and filed away for future use. Anything the target says or does could be used against him or her by the manipulator, and no detail is seen as too small or irrelevant.

Lower Target's Self-Esteem

With the reconnaissance step completed and a thorough understanding of the target achieved, it is time to begin attaching strings, one step at a time. This, first, requires the predator to begin chipping away at the target's self-esteem. Little by little, the manipulator will work to teach the target that he or she does not matter and that ultimately, only the manipulators will be acted upon.

Through steps such as subtle digs that will be denied if called out, self-esteem begins to crack. Consider a target that is sensitive about her weight. The predator may look at her disapprovingly if she goes to get a piece of cake for dessert. Even the slightest downward twitch of his eyebrow in disapproval could be enough to convey his thought, and she is left feeling self-conscious and judged. If she were to call him out, however, he would deny it, saying she imagined the look and that he cannot control what she puts into her body. This may be seen with a hint of patronization within his voice, though, further sending minute, nonverbal cues of his disapproval. As she is sensitive about her weight, she takes his disapproval of her food choices as disapproval of her weight, which chips at her self-esteem. The manipulator may not care about her weight at all, but recognize that it is one of the easiest ways to erode that sense of self she has into something raw enough that metaphorical strings can easily be installed.

The manipulator does not hold back at this stage. Things may be said or implied that cause serious, irreparable harm to the victim through instilling feelings of worthlessness or unworthiness, or implying that the victim is irrevocably broken beyond what any normal human would ever want in a partner. No matter the harm, and no matter the reaction of the individual feeling it, the manipulator will continue. The entire purpose is to degrade the person down into nothing so the manipulator can build her back up again.

This degradation, however, is not overt. As the entire purpose of covert manipulation is to be underhanded, the target feels as though these shifts in personality are entirely unrelated to the predator. The target may begin feeling as though she has to lose weight to be seen as valuable, or an individual who, through a series of small comments meant to cause unease without overtly saying there is a problem, may begin to feel unintelligent or unable to think. Even through simple quirks of a brow, twitches of a smirk or even the pattern in which the manipulator breathes can send unconscious messages to the target that impact the target's line of thought.

Get Results

With the person thoroughly broken, the manipulator can now start training the target into behaving in ways that are desired. Because the target's own self-esteem is now nonexistent, deferring to the manipulator's whims seems natural. The target's very personality has been shifted away from what it was into something that thinks, breathes, and moves in the way that the manipulator desires, and she thinks that those thoughts are her own.

Even just moving in certain ways could be enough for a predator to cue to a brainwashed target to behave in a certain way, and the target will think the move is voluntary. If done well and thoroughly, the target never realizes that there are any strings controlling his or her behaviors, and sees every move, every completed action as being done of his or her own volition. This is key, as the fact that the manipulation was done covertly means that the target never notices it is there, making them a proper source of satisfying whatever whims the predator may have.

Examples of Covert Manipulation

Imagine this situation between the new couple, Amanda and Ben: Amanda is quiet whereas Ben is typically far more assertive and demanding. He is frequently described as a real go-getter, whereas Amanda is more of a people-pleaser. Amanda and Ben have not been dating for very long, but so far, Amanda has felt like Ben is very good at listening to her. She feels that he is quite attentive to her thoughts and feelings, and she feels validated because of this. She is already quite fond of Ben, though she frequently has feelings of not being good enough for him. He has never said or implied that, as far as she is aware.

Soon after they have started getting comfortable with each other, she begins to notice that he is constantly watching her. She tells herself that it is just because he cares, and he confirms that sentiment. She does, however, begin watching what she eats and making sure that she always does her makeup and hair every morning, even if she has no intentions of going anywhere on that particular day. As she gets up earlier to accommodate this new routine, she tells herself that if her boyfriend is going to be looking at her, she has to look good for him. He never asks her to do this or does anything other than watching her. Not too long after, Ben loudly voices his displeasure with a certain group of people, insisting that he feels they do not belong in their country. Amanda does not share this sentiment and feels uncomfortable with her boyfriend talking in such a manner, but does nothing to correct it or call him out. For the next several months, when Ben tells a negative story, he makes sure to associate it with that particular group of people, though subtly. After a while, Amanda begins to associate that particular group of people with negative feelings and negative stories, thus beginning her own instilled biases against the group.

The next time they run into people involved with that particular group, Amanda unconsciously shies away from them, getting closer to Ben, who of course, takes notice of the behavior. He has covertly manipulated her into sharing specific worldviews with him, as well as to make sure that she is dressed up every day, and dieting to slim down to be the perfect arm candy. Consider a second example. A mother named Martha and her adult son named Noah typically spend every weekend together. Every single time that Noah has had to cancel on Martha, she sighs and says that they can try again some other time. She always has that little sigh that makes him feel guilty about missing their usually scheduled time together, and because he feels guilty, he oftentimes tries to make it up to her by inviting her to a nice dinner or bringing her favorite tiramisu for dessert the next time they do get together.

Eventually, Martha begins inserting that little sigh that has been used repeatedly to play with his emotions into other contexts. Sometimes, if she has to do the dishes, she may sigh a little bit to herself before getting up to do them. Oftentimes, Noah responds by getting up and insisting his mother rest while he takes care of the cleanup. If she takes him out to lunch, she may make that little sigh as the bill comes to the table, but plays it off as though she is tired when Noah unconsciously reaches for his own wallet to pay for the meal, whether he could afford it or not.

Any time that Martha shows any signs of unhappiness or displeasure, Noah feels obligated to try to fix it for her, though he does not even realize it himself. He has been manipulated into putting his mother's feelings and comfort before his own, and she absolutely capitalizes on it. He may bring a girlfriend over to meet his mother, but his mother sighs repeatedly during their meeting, sending Noah the signals that she does not approve. He then decides to break up with his girlfriend, though he is never quite sure why or what happened. He simply understands that he has lost interest for some reason. He cannot help but look at her and feel displeased and maybe even a little uncomfortable, though he does not understand why. This is a result of his mother's covert manipulation.

Chapter 3: Dark Persuasion

Persuasion happens everywhere in day-to-day life. It can be seen in how we interact with others, leaning in to persuade people to keep talking while ignoring them in hopes that they will be persuaded to go away. We persuade others to help by asking them and pleading our case, or we persuade people to do something through suggesting it. What makes persuasion dark versus regular persuasion, and how does dark persuasion work? If you want to understand why dark persuasion is so manipulative, you must first understand what it entails, as well as how it differs from harmless persuasion.

Defining Dark Persuasion

At its simplest, persuasion is the act of coaxing or influencing someone into doing or believing something that they did not do or believe prior. Think of asking someone to do something that would never have occurred to them before. Perhaps you ask your partner to help you carry something because it is too heavy, and your partner has not yet offered help. If your partner then decides to carry something for you, you have successfully persuaded them. There is nothing inherently manipulative or wrong about doing this—you are simply asking for help and your partner obliges.

Dark persuasion, then, adds a level of darkness. Remember, darkness implies selfishness or harm, as discussed in the first section of this book. The propensity for darkness is the propensity to doing things for one's own selfish interest with no regard of what it may or may not do to those around the manipulator. They do not care if people get hurt, betrayed, or upset. The only thing that matters to people who have a propensity for darkness or dark psychology is that one's own wants and needs are met.

Taking those two definitions, of darkness and of persuasion, you can then infer that dark persuasion is the art of influencing people to act in a way that is primarily or only beneficial to the manipulator with no regard for those being manipulated. Anything that the manipulator attempts to get from others is selfishly motivated. This selfishness, this darkness, is what makes dark persuasion so dangerous or harmful to others.

Persuasion vs. Dark Persuasion

If persuasion is acceptable, but dark persuasion is harmful, what is the real difference, you may ask. The difference lies in the intention. Persuasion, by and large, does not seek to inflict harm, and if anything, often seeks to better both the person doing the persuading and the person being persuaded. Oftentimes when trying to persuade someone, you are doing so because you believe it would be better, and this is from a good spot, seeking to benefit the other person as well. You are not trying to convince the other person to do something for your own benefit, and only your own benefit.

Ultimately, the one-sided selfishness is what differentiates the two from each other. Persuasion is not necessary but can be, selfish, but dark persuasion always is. Dark persuasion is almost always one-sided, though the other person may believe there is some sort of benefit to him or her as well. In contrast, persuasion often seeks to balance benefits of all involved, attempting to spread as much good as possible. All parties involved in normal persuasion usually benefit in some way, shape, or form, but only the manipulator benefits in dark persuasion. Dark persuasion does not concern itself with morality, whereas persuasion does. The dark persuader does not care about right or wrong, but the persuader does.

How Dark Persuasion Works

Persuasion, and therefore dark persuasion, works through seven elements. These elements enable you to influence other people, no matter whether you seek to genuinely persuade someone with the best of intentions or you wish to darkly persuade someone into the behavior you know they would not necessarily care for. Understanding these seven elements is crucial to understanding exactly how to persuade others.

Reciprocity

Reciprocity is the idea that when someone helps or gives you something, you should return the favor. Even if it is as simple as someone smiling at you, you should smile back. No matter how big or small, the favor should be returned. This typically works in everyone's favor when everyone reciprocates, because everyone sees benefits. If Alice asks Brenda for help moving furniture in exchange for homemade cookies and Brenda agrees to do so, the next time that Brenda needs help with something, Alice is going to be more likely to volunteer or agree to help. We inherently want to help others who help us; it is part of our wiring as a social species.

However, this idea of reciprocity also applies in dark persuasion. If you seek to tap into dark persuasion, you are going to seek to create a sense of obligation in your target. You will do something for the other person with the intent of cashing in on the favor you feel you are owed. Many people are likely to give in to this notion, as well, and will oftentimes, even if begrudgingly, attempt to reciprocate.

The idea with dark manipulation is to offer a small favor, typically something that does not take much of your time or energy, and then shortly after, request a favor in return. The shorter the time between you doing a favor and asking for a favor, the more likely it is that the answer will be yes, even with favors that are exponentially larger. For example, if you offer to cover your friend's coffee, insisting it is no big deal when you know that he is struggling with money while you are out, you can turn around and ask your friend to help you by babysitting all evening while you go out on a date with your spouse. The reciprocity is not even between the two—all you did was buy a cheap coffee, but you are asking your friend to give up several hours in return. Say your date is set to last four hours, and you spent $3.50 on the coffee: This is essentially paying your friend the equivalent of $0.88/hour if you were to calculate out work for pay. This may sound like a fantastic price to pay for childcare for you, but your friend ends up caring for your children for well below minimum wage, and is honestly, probably at a loss after factoring in food that the children will inevitably ask for during a four-hour window. At this point, your friend, who is already struggling to make ends meet, actually lost some money in return for drinking a cheap mocha from a café.

Consistency and Commitment

Consistency is important within persuasion because of three key factors: It is valued, creates a schedule that can be used to manage all of one's many responsibilities, and it can simplify situations that are otherwise difficult to juggle due to having a routine. This means that consistency, in effect, makes people's daily tasks more streamlined. People are able to get through everything easier when they have a set routine that enables them to meet all of their responsibilities that has proven effective in the past.

The consistency in routine allows for reliability as well. Someone who is consistent is typically also quite reliable because of his or her routine. Therefore, someone who is consistent becomes easy to persuade. One that person has agreed to do something for you, you can be certain they will follow through due to their own skills at self-motivating to remain consistent. In dark persuasion, you can take this to mean that once someone who is consistent has said they will do something, they will motivate themselves to do so, even if, halfway through, they realize that it is something that they have no desire to do, or is something that does not quite line up with their own belief systems.

Going hand-in-hand with consistency comes commitment. Those who are consistent typically follow through with commitments no matter what. They self-motivate to get the job done due to their consistency. Those who have proven themselves consistent typically will continue to follow that pattern, believing remaining consistent and reliable is integral to which they are as a person. This self-motivation is, in essence, a form of self-persuasion. By simply getting a commitment, you may not even have to do the persuasion part; the other person will do the work for you.

This means that once you bind this person to do something, it will almost absolutely happen. Commitments are valued and not taken lightly. Even if you do find that the other person is balking at the agreement and seeming as though he or she may back out of the arrangement, appealing to that commitment, reminding the other person that they had promised or otherwise committed him- or herself to completing the commitment is often enough to keep them in line.

Within dark persuasion, then, by earning a commission, particularly from someone consistent, you are able to then ensure that you do not have to work hard to hold the other person accountable. Ultimately, those interested in dark persuasion and covert manipulation seek to get results with the least amount of effort, so by getting someone that you know is consistent and dedicated to meeting commitments, you are able to lessen your workload. You know that you are not likely to need to nag at the other person to follow through, which means you do not have to do as much follow up work.

Social Proof

Social proof is, in essence, herd mentality. It is the idea that people feel the constraints of social pressure demanding that they act in a certain way. It is the feeling of being obligated to do something simply because society dictates that is the way things are done, particularly in situations in which someone is unfamiliar. When unsure about the situation, people tend to follow the lead of those around them, feeling the pressure to conform. They assume that those around them, who seem to be moving around seamlessly, know what is supposed to be done, and therefore decide to mimic them in hopes of behaving appropriately.

This phenomenon is even more pronounced when the individual who is unsure about the situation is able to closely relate to those who are acting, to whom the individual decides to conform. This can be seen in various experiments. In one such experiment, researchers joined a charity campaign that went door to door to get donations. When the list of donators had more names on it, the people being asked to donate were typically more likely to donate, particularly when the person being solicited recognized names on the donor list as being known neighbors, friends, or peers.

This relates to persuasion because it involves what is seen as horizontal rather than vertical; at its core, this means that people are more likely to be influenced by their peers than their superiors. They are more likely to adopt the behaviors of people they identify with than those who have power.

Within dark persuasion, then, this concept could be used to influence people to conform. If the predator were to fabricate a list of donators, for example, he would be able to better convince people to donate. Likewise, the predator could fabricate situations in which the target is alongside people who are acting the way the predator desires, allowing for the predator to influence the target's actions without it ever becoming obvious.

Likable

Imagine that two people, one who you like, and the others who you do not, ask you to do the same thing. Who do you help, if anyone? The most likely answer is that you will help the person you like. People tend to agree to help people they like and are far more likely to say yes if they like the person attempting to persuade them. The question, then, is who do people like? How do people decide who the like and dislike? Ultimately, the answer involves three factors that determine how likable someone is to us:

- People with whom we can identify closely
- People who complement or flatter us
- People who are willing to cooperate in order to attain similar, mutual goals or outcomes

Understanding what people like and naturally gravitate toward gives manipulators an idea of how to act in order to get inside a desired target's inner circle. The manipulator learns that, in order to get a yes, he or she should aim to be relatable, compliment the target, and identify common goals, even if those common goals are falsified by the manipulator to create some sort of semblance of a connection.

Once those three standards have been met, the dark persuader is far more likely to get desired results when asking someone to do something. The persuader has tapped into unconscious biases and tendencies in order to get desired results.

Authority

By and large, people defer to authority and are more likely to do whatever someone asks if they see clear signs of authority presented to them. For example, a person may listen to what a nurse has to say about care at home, but may not follow through. If that same person were told the same thing by a doctor whose lab coat declared them the head of the ER department, however, they would be far more likely to do as told. This is because the person unconsciously defers to higher authorities. In the person's mind, the nurse may not be as worthy of being an authority as the doctor who is the head of the emergency room, even though the information provided is exactly the same.

In terms of being able to persuade others, then, this implies that it is important to cue that the predator is an authority in some way. You can convince people to buy products if you have a business degree hanging on the wall, and you can sway someone by using your credentials with your name on nameplates, business cards, and other identifying items. Consider if someone talked to you about what you should do with your insurance on your car—would you be more inclined to listen to a random person in casual clothes, or someone wearing a shirt emblazoned with the logo of a popular, well-known insurance company? The answer is the one who has identified themselves as a representative of an insurance company. You would assume they are an authority on the product if their shirt marks them as someone involved with the insurance business.

The dark persuaders, then, could take this a step further. Either through misrepresenting experience, or even lying about credentials, they are able to be seen as more reliable. They may discuss some reason they have more working knowledge over a situation, and because of that, they should be seen as a default authority on the matter.

Scarcity

People always want what they cannot have. Because oftentimes, people see the proverbial grass is greener on the other side, by imposing scarcity on a product, demand goes up. If an unpopular item is being removed from a menu, people will suddenly want it more, until it is gone, at which point, that item that never sold well in the first place is suddenly missed. Many restaurants follow similar structures, offering items for a limited time only, although realistically, they would be able to produce enough to meet demand if they chose to. Hype for the item is built through the exclusive nature of it—because it is limited, more people want to try it before they lose the opportunity forever.

When it comes to persuading others, then, keeping scarcity in mind can be particularly useful. Not only should a predator make sure to tout benefits toward what people can gain by going along with the predator's plan, but also what may be lost if the plan is not followed. Emphasizing the temporary nature of the deal, as well as what the loss of the deal will entail. People will be far more likely to go along with the plan if they feel like they stand to lose something if they do not do it.

Chapter 4: Dark Persuasion and Covert Manipulation particular aspects

As you have understood the concept of dark persuasion and covert manipulation in the previous chapter, now it's time to know some other aspects of them. As in the above paragraphs, you have clearly understood what persuasion is. The difference between dark persuasion and persuasion is of intentions. A persuader always tries to convince through particular techniques or motivation without having any sort of understanding about the person whom they are trying to convince. He is only concerned about doing good for people and thinking of their benefit along with their own. He does everything with a good intention without too many facts and figures of the person whom they are trying to convince.

On the other hand, dark persuader also thinks and analyzes a bigger picture. They very well understand that what are the tactics they need to use to succeed and how far do they need to take it. They only think that they are doing something right but are unconcerned with the morality of manipulation he does. They always try to achieve whatever they want through any means whichever the feel can be more effective.

Persuasion is never without moral implications but in dark persuasion moral implications are just not the determining factor. There are many other factors which are more important than being morally correct. The smartest thing about a dark persuader is that in their circle they would be the most selfish person but would show and seem that they are least selfish. They would get exactly what they get, without the other person knowing or even realizing.

The other thing that a dark persuader does is knowing about the weakness of others. This helps them in extracting words, presents, and gifts which they can take or give according to their advantage and situation. For example, if an employer knows that he has illegal immigrants working in his company, he can always lower his wages as per his choice as they know that they cannot work anywhere else in the country.

Dark persuasion can vary from small to very large scale, such as a kid asking his elder brother for all the ice cream he has to a leader trying to ask for help in war to defeat another country. So, to determine dark persuasion it is always vital to understand the different personalities and their circumstances.

Covert manipulation is even worse than manipulation, in this, the manipulator tries to use the emotional vulnerability to their benefit. They would strive to their best so that they can know about your goals, strengths, weaknesses, fear, family, etc. So that they can use all of these factors to make you feel low and weak. It is said to be underhanded methods of control. It operates under your level of conscious awareness. The bad part of it is that the victim is not even aware that they are being manipulated, that is the reason it becomes prime for you to know about the manipulation games that these people use, which we will discuss later in coming chapters.

Covert manipulation is very dangerous as it is so subtle and underhanded that it takes a long time before you can make out that you were being manipulated. According to research, it was also found that there are few manipulators with such sharp skills that they are called puppet masters, you would without even knowing become their puppets, so it is important for you to know their signs so that you can take the actions accordingly. They would make you feel that you are doing according to your own wish but the truth is that you do that only what they ask you to do.

Sometimes you might feel that something is wrong but you would not be able to analyze that someone is trying to manipulate you. In covert manipulation first thing which is prime is that you should ask yourself if you are being manipulated? As covert manipulation is adverse and has a negative effect on us, so it would be easier for you to understand that you are being manipulated.

It is significant for you to understand a few characteristics of a covert manipulator, so it becomes really easy for you to spot them if they are around you-

1) Lying- They would lie straight in your eyes and you would not even get to know that they are lying. They would tell you twisted truth or half-truth which you might or might not get to know later. If you ever have any doubts on the other person about the truth, you should always double-check the information so that it does not hamper your relationship or work.

2) Backhanded compliments- This is something they are best at. Covert manipulators are great in giving backhanded compliments. They would give compliments as you did it in a great way although you are so weak and low in confidence, still, you handled it well. You cooked so well, although you do not cook for me often. These compliments make you feel even more embarrassed and awkward, where you do not even know how to react. In such cases, the best thing is to ignore or giving them the taste of their own medicine by replying in the same way.

3) Mirroring- The coincidences would be extravagant. They would agree to all your points, likes, dislikes, taste, color, etc just to impress you or to be with you. When they want to take benefit from you they would agree to all your things and choices. Once they get what they wanted everything would change. You would feel that the person has fully switched. So, you should always beware of the person who agrees to whatever you say without keeping their point of you, it straight away means that they are trying to be manipulative.

4) Rationalization- This is something many people would do to cover their lies or fault. They would cook new stories to cover their flaws such as the reason why you did not tell that you had a girlfriend before me, the reason they would give you would be like I did not want to lose you by telling this or I did not know how you would react after listening to this, etc. Thu they would have answers for all the lies, so make sure that you know and follow your gut feel to analyze if he is saying right or just faking it.

5) Hurried Intimacy- This is a very alarming sign of a covert manipulator. They would very quickly tell you about their goals, achievements, passion and past and what ask you the same things. Once you open up with them, they would use this information to control and manipulate you. Therefore, you should always be wise enough to understand when to share the information and how much information to share. They would be very quick in proposing for marriage and talking about the future but you need to be careful before telling your weaknesses.

6) Playing the victim- This is another thing they do to gain your sympathy. Just to gain your love and attention they would lie to you to any extent. They might say that their childhood was very bad as the parents were not good, etc. Just to get more love and care from you. They might make any stories for your love and care, so always know the past first before you get so much involved.

7) Silent Treatment- Leaving room or house for a couple of hours, would not engage in any activity, etc. They also hide behaviors or start avoiding you so that you realize it is your mistake or you start the conversation. They keep the concerns unspoken within them which is a dangerous sign too.

8) Belittling- They do react weird such as rolling the eyes, scoffing, mocking, teasing, etc. They do not even respect others point of view or abilities, and they always want another person to feel low and always try to demean them. You should always maintain a distance with such covert people who are jealous of your success and feel bad seeing you rise.

9) Word Play- A covert manipulator very well knows what you want to hear and would please your ears by saying that. They know how to put a convincing statement, paint the picture well and also to induce an emotional reaction in front of you. Not only this, they are great it talking double meaning things, they would mean something else but say it in a different context. For example, please marry me I will change your life. This can be in any aspect positive or negative. So be precise and clear while talking to a covert manipulator.

10) Finance controller- Covet manipulator not only restrict by playing with your emotions they are also good in controlling and gaming with your finances too. For example, accessing your account but denying access to their account, taking things on loan in joint names without even asking you, running up debts, borrowing and not paying, etc. These are very tricky things which you should be careful about and take a step in time before they make your account nil.

These were the few characteristics of a covert manipulator which you should be diligent about so that nobody can take advantage of you or humiliate you.

Chapter 5: Signs that your Partner is Manipulating You

When you get attached to someone you love the way they are and are also happily accepting than the same way. But there are times when it becomes important for you to change a few things in you and some in your partner for the betterment of your relationship. There are times in a relationship when you start thinking that your partner has stopped caring about you, has become self-centered or started imposing things on you. There are small things initially that you would think as cute such as cooking good food for your husband and telling him over dinner that you hit the car when you went out. At times it is fine, but slowly if these things turn darker and deeper it can be a big concern for you.

Manipulation starts from the ground level and can reach up to the sky. It is you who have to set the limits and understand when these small things turn into bigger ones. You should always have the confidence to speak up and stand against something which is not right and against your wish. You should always yourself a question that does you have that much courage to say no when you do not want to do something. Manipulative people particularly choose the partners who can be easily manipulated as they like things to happen their own way.

But these manipulative people are really wise and would not let you see these signs at the beginning of the relationship. You should always be vigilant in your relationship and if you observe that small threats are turning into bigger ones and if you do not agree to what they say, the big angry or aggressive, it is a clear sign that you are with a manipulative partner. As if your partner does not respect your decision even after you explain your reasons clearly to them and still try to do things according to wish it means that they are selfish and are not concerned about what you want from life.

Manipulators just do not change overnight. It is just that their small demands get bigger day by day and their tolerance of accepting 'no' gets smaller with each passing day. All of your time might pass by thinking whether you want to be in this relationship or not. The thoughts that come to your mind confuse you where one side you might think that love means giving and on the other side you might think that love should be unconditional. But believe me, if you want to spend your life happy, peacefully and according to your wishes, then coming out of the relationship is substantial for you. You might feel difficult saying no and staying without your partner but it will make your life easy and you would be able to live it according to your own terms.

At times, people are just not able to say no because they have fear in their mind that how would they react when you will say no. Forget about your people-pleasing behavior, think about yourself, when you would stop bending over to make everyone happy, then is the time you would feel confident and be who you are. Now you know that is crucial to take s step when you got to know that your partner is manipulative. But let us first understand well about the signs of a manipulative lover-

•They provoke you- When they have nothing to say and are out of the argument, they would provoke you. They might do things which would make you angry and trigger your negative emotions. The only purpose to do is that they want you to indulge in a pointless quarrel so that they can use something in their defense. If you feel that they are unnecessarily exaggerating and poking you, the best thing to do is just calm down, and try to stay on the topic. If you are unable to do that, then just try and end the discussion politely.

•They know how to use tricks- They are always ready with their dirty tricks to get what they want. They would request for you big things in such a way that they are asking for some small favors. They are very clever and know how to deal with different kinds of people. For example, they would say that if we cannot go to a far off restaurant for dinner, then let us just go to a nearby restaurant for eating Chinese food. The only option they would leave for you is to select the easier one. But you should not come up in their tricks as it is not always important to help and you should help if you want to, not because they are providing with options.

•Gaslighting Technique- In this method they try to distort the past and twist the facts so that it would confuse you. They would ask questions like, Did I not call you? Why would I not call you when I know you need me? They would be so confident and sure that you start doubting your own memory. They very well know which point is to be used when. To get rid of this wicked tactic you should always trust your memory and tell them that you remember what you said. This way they would either stop using this technique or at least beware that you remember very well what you say and do.

•Pressurize you- Everyone knows if you have less time to make decisions, you would not be able to see all the aspects of the situation. This is what manipulators do in a relationship. They would always push you to make decisions faster by giving you less time when they do not want you to think over something very much. So, it is always good to ask for some time, so that you can see the pros and cons of t according to you and check if it suits you. If they still want you to hurry, then politely just answer that you are thinking about it and need some time to take the decision.

•Emotional blackmail- This is a very common sign of a manipulator, they are really good at emotionally blackmailing you. They always try to you the weakest point of you and show insecurity by saying statements like, I will die without you or I cannot live without you, etc. They try to threaten their health and life but do not take it too seriously as it is just a threat. Also, if they say something like this, just tell them whatever they do, you would not be responsible for it.

•You are the one who is guilty and they are the victims- Manipulators in a relationship would always show that it is your mistake and they are the ones who are the victims because of it. They would always make you guilt by saying- you know I have so much work in an office, stop being selfish, etc. which would make you feel guilty. But do not feel that way; stay calm and make them realize that they are responsible for their behavior. They avoid responsibility and just try to become victims by showing that are insecure and get benefit from you. They do such things to gain attention from you so that your love and concern for them increases. But you need to be prepared and know when to pay attention and when to avoid.

•Avoid discussions- Manipulators mostly avoid discussing common problems between both of you or family-related. They would always try to end the discussion before it starts or not even to listen to what you want to say. For this, you should always make sure that you stick to your point and make them understand that it is important and clear it out.

Changing a manipulator is very difficult as it is a trait of character. These people are difficult to change as they love sticking to it even if it costs you being separated. It is always good to take this step if you do not see any change in the person because it is always good to take trouble once rather than elongating it for your whole life. Separating, divorce or break-up are not small words. All these things take a lot of courage and time and before taking this decision. There are many things to analyze and see if your decision is right. It is just not simple to just ask yourself what are you being the victim of manipulation and you get the answer.

No, it does not work that way, first, you have to start realizing things. Once you realize then only you can find out the ways of coming out of the trap of manipulation. Here is a list of few points which you need to check with yourself and see if you feel that way, then it is the time to take a stand for yourself-

•Accountability- You always think that you have an obligation towards your partner. You think that you are solely responsible for keeping them happy or sad. You don't know the reason but you feel grateful towards that they are in your life. If you have such kind of burden on your mind and that they make you feel accountable for all the actions and also say that it depends on you how their mood is and how they react. In these kinds of situations, you should always start taking a step back and see if they feel the same way. Stop feeling grateful that they love you as you do them the same way.

•Fear- If you fear their awkward pauses when you are trying to say no, please stop getting scared. If your partner asks you to do something and when you want to say no but when they stare at you, you lose your courage and do as they say. This is a sign that you do not have freedom in your relationship which is why you do not have the courage to speak up. There is no point in being a relationship where you cannot open up and keep your opinion. You should either have the courage to speak up and still if things do not get better, then move out.

•Justification- If you have to give justification for every action you take and do not have the right to choose for yourself, you are not with the right person. Also, you should not justify yourself by thinking that you are dependent on them and they know better. Do not let these excuses make a web around you. Be brave and confident to know what is best for you and do not feel that you need anyone to make decisions for you. Wait for the reaction and face it boldly.

•Anxiety- This is the cause of concern in many relationships, you feel anxious whenever you are with them. You feel very anxious when they start talking to you or ask for a favor. There might be fear in your mind that they might not ask you for something which you cannot do and also cannot say no. This type of relationship is like a snare in which you are stuck and do not know what to do. All you need here is to understand that if you cannot speak up today, then how will you stand for your values in the near future. So always instead of feeling anxious either say no or tell them what you feel. This is the only solution for a healthy relationship and health. Else the only option left with you is to break up.

•Increased Expectations- Manipulative people are greedy and always want more and more. You give them as much as you can and they still would urge more from you. They would be happy and pleased to see your efforts but still, they would have more expectations more you. If you feel the same with your partner and think that you are loaded with too much of demands and expectations. It is the time to clear it in your head first that do as much as you can; it is not important to go the extra mile to please your partner.

•Started hating yourself- You start hating yourself by thinking that you are weak and cannot face these kinds of situation. You know that your partner is taking advantage of you being nice but still, you do not have the strength to tell that on their face or walk-off from their life. Instead of hating yourself, read books, do not fight- just discuss and come out of the trap.

Thus, be careful while you are in a relationship and take decision accordingly. Do not rush or think it's too late. There is always time to improve and come out of any relationship. So if someone is trying to manipulate you in a relationship, give them a chance and if it does not work then take your step.

Chapter 6: Victims of Manipulation

Before we talk about the victims of manipulation, the first thing that might come to your mind is why do people manipulate? There can be numerous reasons why people choose the way of manipulation instead of persuasion. The first thing can be that they do not know the difference between them. Second and the major reason is when people do not have the skills to achieve something in the right manner and feel helpless and hopeless then they start to manipulate people. Also, there is this fear of being left out or being abandoned because of which just to gain the attention they think that manipulation can play a good role.

Next reason can be when they want to control and dominate others for that they start using their anger, aggression, being extra sweet, etc. They use all the techniques of manipulation to get the work done from you. Another thing can be when they want to raise their self-esteem and lower yours they use wicked tricks to be in good books of their seniors and want to show that you are weak and less-knowledgeable than them.

Manipulators have all the negative thoughts in their mind when they use these techniques as they never do anything for the benefit of others as they are very self-centered. It is always good to maintain a distance from such kind of people as they are very difficult to handle. If you are in such a situation when people like these cannot be completely avoided, you should always consider your security above everything.

Also, be honest and direct with these sorts of people and ask questions straight away from their expectations from you. Never feel guilty or ashamed of any work you do if it is right as these people find reasons humiliate you. But the best thing you can do to them is to avoid and ignore. The other thing about these manipulators is that they know who to make their victim.

Skilled manipulators know very well what to look for to make someone their victim. For them, people who like meeting the needs of everyone and like pleasing others are the easiest people to target. They choose them as they are easy to manipulate, victimize and blame. Also, people who do not say no or does not know how to say no are the other targets of the manipulators as these people would do what they say without any trouble.

Other victims for them are people who have less confidence as those people are very easy to mould and convince, they choose them to get their work done. Also, people who do not know how to speak out, keep their opinion and fight back are the best prey for them. Manipulators very well know whom they can benefit from and who are the people to stay away from. Anyone can be a victim of manipulation you or me, sometimes small threats and at times big too. Being a victim is bad but not giving it back is even worse. You should always have the courage to give it back or walk out when you know that someone is taking undue advantage of you.

Let us see how can you cut the wings of a manipulator if you are the victim-

1) Analyze your mind- Manipulation only happens when we let it happen. Yes, there are few things in life which we have no control over but manipulation is not the one. If you think that someone is trying to play dirty manipulation tricks with you the first thing you should do is analyze what is your role in the manipulation process. If you think that yes you are being manipulated, then you are the one who can stop it there and then. Sometimes you do not feel comfortable facing the situation and saying straight away no, in that case, ensure that you would not say yes too. You should recognize the ability in yourself of controlling your reactions and handling the situation.

2) Know what is important- Things become complicated and you get manipulated when you do for others and know what is important for them. So, it is crucial for you to first understand what you want to do and what is your aim. Know what matters to you the most, then only you would be able to say no to others and focus on your path. Then you would have a reason to say no the manipulator as a no without a reason would give a chance to manipulator to question you.

3) Ask for transparency- As by now it is very much clear to all of us that manipulators play games which we have discussed in previous chapters, so they are excellent at selling their point of view and getting their work done. But you should also act smartly and always ask how you would benefit by that. If they are wrong, you would be able to judge that by seeing their reactions and they might even fumble. As they might not be expecting that you would ask, they are not prepared for the answer. The reason behind it is that manipulators always think about themselves and are not concerned about your interest in it. Also, when you start asking questions about your interest they would understand that you cannot be their victim anymore and would change their target.

4) Stay adamant- There are times when it might be very strenuous for you to come out of the control of the skilled manipulators as they are very good at controlling people. They would be charming, manipulative and determined to let you down and keep you under their control. All these aspects would make it difficult for you to handle them but you have to be adamant and cut the strings of the manipulator by showing them that you are strong and confident and can very well understand their dirty tricks.

These were the few tips to take out manipulators from your life and identifying people who are creating a mess in our life. It is not possible for us to stand for ourselves till the time we do not believe in us and start loving ourselves. Firstly, you not to know that you are capable and strong and others cannot fool you in any way. So just stay true to your values and always vow to do better in your life.

When you become a victim of a manipulator be it your partner, friend, colleague or boss it really hurts at times and there might be some adverse effects on you of it. Your mind gets really disturbed as things you have not thought of might happen. Emotional manipulation can also lead to problems like trust, intimacy, security, belief, trust and many other issues like this which may have more short and long term effects on you. The scars of them might not be physically seen but stay within you sometimes for even a lifetime. Let us know some of the effects of manipulation on the victims-

Short Term Effects

• Avoid eye contact- Because of a lack of confidence and low-esteem, the victims start to avoid eye contact with people. Victims start feeling small from inside and feel insecure that they do not become a victim for some other manipulator, so they try to avoid eye contact and conversation with people

• Cautious and anxious- They get so broken from inside that to avoid any sort of manipulation In the future, they become extra cautious towards themselves and others both. Victims become too much careful and watchful about others behavior and start doubting them, which even makes it difficult for them to make friends. They are also anxious all the time just thinking whom to trust and whom to not.

• Confused- They also get in a state of shock thinking that a person who was so dear to them how can he change and manipulate them like this. They stay confused and in deep thought just analyzing what and how it happened. Victims sometimes even cannot believe and are confused that this can happen to them, this can be both a long term and short term effect.

- Guilt- Victims might also feel hateful about themselves and guilty as to why did they not get to know about them before. Why were they not able to recognize the manipulators and let them take you for granted. Questions might this arise in your mind but you have to be strong and trust yourself. So do not blame yourself as they are skilled manipulators and they are well aware of your weaknesses and how to take advantage of it.

- Be overcautious- As they have faced so much in the past they become extra cautious while talking to others so that the other person does not get upset or angry about anything you do. This behavior of the victims makes them think a lot which makes them anxious and too much stressed.

• Self-questioning- You start questioning yourself about the past things and whatever you do in the present too. You try to think if you recall everything the same way it happened or not. This happens because manipulators question you for each and everything you do or at times also make you realize that you do not remember things right. So in every situation, you meet feel doubtful about yourself but you need to trust yourself and move on.

Long-term Effects

• Feeling hateful- You might feel irritated, impatience and frustration. All these factors inculcate within you after being manipulated. When someone treats you in a bad manner, it becomes really tough to take it out from your mind. You start feeling resentful and hating others too.

• Depressed- You start feeling depressed especially when you have been emotionally manipulated. You have been told so many lies that your trust breaks to such an extent that you start feeling depressed and it seems difficult for you to come out of it. But you do not need to worry, it may be a long term effect but it can be healed with time.

• Feeling numb- You feel like staying alone and would stop reacting to things. This numbness is very dangerous and you should always try to stay with your friends or loved ones in this situation. Even in situations which make you happy and content you would not feel good and want to move out of it. You would feel hopeless and broken but do not let one incident become you a victim for a lifetime. Just stay with your closed ones and try to cope up with the situation by reading positive books and watching movies or listen to
music do anything that makes you feel good.

- Too much observant- After being the victim, you start observing and judging things excessively, you may just think of everyone in the same way and judge them accordingly. They would not even try to control you but you would always feel that they want to control you or want to take some benefit out of you but this is not the truth. For this, you would have to let the past go. Yes, you have to be careful, but at least give yourself one more chance.

These were the few effects that have been observed on victims. Be it a long term effect or a short term, it takes time to heal any sort of manipulation. But you should always feel positive about it that they are not in your life anymore. Have faith in you and do not trust people too early, take time to analyze and judge them after that make them your friends and open your heart in front of them.

CPSIA information can be obtained
at www.ICGtesting.com
Printed in the USA
LVHW010724090621
689685LV00005B/844

9 781803 115122